JENTON MENN
D1162319

# YOUR BODY IS YOUR OWN

## A Book for Parents and Children to Read Together

**Written by**
**Amy C. Bahr**

**Illustrated by**
**Frederick**
**Bennett Green**

## GROSSET & DUNLAP

Copyright © 1986 by RGA Publishing Group, Inc. and Frederick Bennett Green. Concept by
RGA Publishing Group, Inc. IT'S OK TO SAY NO is a trademark of RGA Publishing Group, Inc.
Published by Grosset & Dunlap, a member of The Putnam Publishing Group, New York.
Printed in Italy. Published simultaneously in Canada. Library of Congress Catalog
Card Number: 85-080575 ISBN 0-448-15326-2   A B C D E F G H I J

## NOTE TO PARENTS

As responsible parents, we protect our children by teaching them the rules and regulations of water safety, fire safety, and bicycle safety. The IT'S OK TO SAY NO Picture Books will help you teach your child the most important safety lesson of all—body safety.

As you read this book with your child, or with a child you care about, you may want to expand on some of the situations, or you may prefer to read the simple text just as it is. In either case, this book should stimulate discussion. It's important that you take the time to let your child respond to questions asked in the book, and that you listen to any questions the child may have. If you feel awkward or embarrassed, you should direct these questions to someone you and your child feel comfortable with. Above all, the child must understand and remember the rules that will help him or her to recognize and respond to threatening situations.

The IT'S OK TO SAY NO Picture Books are not meant to scare but rather to educate. Children need to learn the words and phrases in the books and use them to say no, to tell their parents if something is wrong, and to avoid dangerous situations. Adults, in turn, must learn to listen and must give their children the freedom to tell.

**—The Children's Justice Foundation, Inc.**

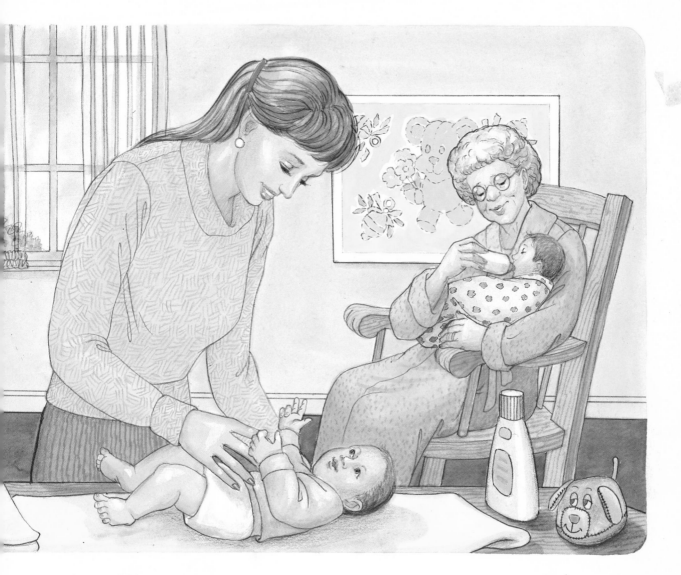

When you were a baby, grownups fed you and dressed you and
changed your diapers. They picked you up and played with you.
They hugged you and kissed you whenever they wanted to.

Now you're not a baby anymore. You can do lots of things for yourself. You can *say* when you want someone to help you and when you don't.

You can say, "Please do my buttons."
You can say, "I'll zip it up myself."
You can say, "I can tie my shoes."

If you fall down and hurt yourself, you can ask your dad to pick you up and hug you. And when you feel better, you can ask him to put you down.

You're not a baby anymore. Your body is your own, and *you* can say who touches it. You might let your parents' friends kiss you when they come over, or you might want to shake hands instead.

You might want to give Grandpa a hug before he leaves, or you might want to blow him a kiss.

It's OK to say so if you don't like the way someone touches you.
If you don't like to be kissed on the mouth, you can say, "Kiss me
on the cheek!"

No one has the right to grab you and play with you unless you say it's OK. Sometimes it's fun to wrestle or be tickled or do tricks.

But if you're not having fun anymore, you can say, "Stop! That's enough." Even the people you love don't always know when you feel uncomfortable. But you can tell them.

Some parts of your body are private. You don't run around with no clothes on the way a baby sometimes does.

You wear a bathing suit when you go to the swimming pool so that your private parts are covered.

It's OK to say that you want some privacy. If you don't need any
help in the bathroom, you say, "I can go by myself."

If you don't want your babysitter to help you put on your pajamas, it's OK to say, "I can do it myself."

Your body belongs to you. If you don't like someone patting your bottom, you should say, "Don't do that anymore!"

If someone tries to touch your private parts, you should say "Leave me alone!" Tell your mom or your dad or another grownup you trust if anyone tries to touch you in a way that makes you feel uncomfortable.

Now that you're older, you can tell the difference between a good touch and a bad touch. A good touch makes you feel happy and warm. A bad touch makes you feel yucky or scared.

No one has the right to touch you in a way that makes you feel uncomfortable. If someone holds onto you when you want her to let you go, that is a bad touch.

If holding hands with your best friend makes you both feel happy, that is a good touch.

If a goodnight kiss helps you feel snug and sleepy, that is a good touch.

If a grownup wants you to touch him in a way that makes you feel weird, that is a bad touch. You should say, "No! I won't!" and get away from him.

If you don't like to be alone with someone because he makes you feel scared or uncomfortable, tell your mom or dad how you feel.

A good touch for someone else might not be a good touch for you. Some people like big bear hugs.

Some people like little butterfly kisses. It's OK to be different.

Everybody needs good touches to make them feel happy and loved. If you need a hug, you can say so.

If you don't like the way someone touches you, you can speak up and tell him to stop.

Now you know that your body is your own!